VERSES' LADDER

RHYTHM BEADED IN WORDS

HARSHITA JAISWAL

ISBN 979-888569315-8

"Gratitude , my Mum, Daddy, Shristi, Shaurya, D , for constantly letting me flourish and to play the skeleton to my structure."

"This peice of writing is dedicated to all the readers."

"

"

Contents

Contents

Contents

Preface

Ever since I dive into world of writing, it has been a process to decipher my mind and heart and discover the art altogether through my pen. The root of this book is an incident happened long back when I was told to explain a saying crafted on board by my teacher followed by my mum constantly reminding me to get better and compile the records. I had been longing for a medium to open my inner self and discovered writing and in no time it became my utmost asset.

This book is the beginning of a journey. This book offers an understanding of one's different aspect of living whether it is an act of repentance, a lithe life, stressed running individual or beauty of hope. What better way can there be to get introduced to the world of rhythm than a poetry? This is what this book offers. This book can play a role of window in your mind to enter in the world of, not so confined genre, poetry. Furthermore I would like to affix that I own every statement retorted in this book and reflects my thoughts only.

I hope this book triggers your eagerness for reading.

Acknowledgements

Writing this book is an experience of discovering my pen. I would like to grasp this very opportunity to thank everyone involve in my journey of discovering the art and encouraging to step on the ladder , my Mum, Daddy, Shristi, Shaurya, D.

1. Space Inside Me

The one which is reflecting,
The other which is hidden,
In between the contradiction,
Here "I Am."
Once you peep inside,
Twice you going to interrogate,
Or fluster thrice to know
All the flaws I foster till date,
What "I Am."
I may feint a lot to fend worries
But glad to meet to hurdles
Every week.
In order to get along with gays,
I pamper my strength.
And pull my shoes beneath
That's how "I Am."
I may fall feeble there
And fought with giggles here,
After a heavy day
That seems to be real,
I finally lay down in
"SPACE INSIDE ME."

2. YOU AND ME

YOU BEING ECONOMIC WITH TRUTH,
ME BELIEVING THE CHARACTERS IN FRONT,
NOW, WHICHEVER WAY THIS SELF GOES,
IS MORE OF A WAR BETWEEN ME AND YOU.
YOU ARE CLOSEST TO SELF,
BUT ME IS WHAT WE ENTRUST THE MOST.
THE BIZZARE LOOK THAT SELF IS IN,
IS EVEN SCARIER FOR MIRROR TO REFLECT.
YOU ARE SHATTER AND I AM JAM,
CONCLUSIVE STATEMENT IS YET TO MAKE.
NOT ALL YOU'S CAN LEAD TO GOAL,
NOT ALL ME'S ARE SUPPOSE TO BE FOE,
YOU ARE LOGICAL,
ME BEING ILLOGICALY INSANE.
IT'S A NEVER ENDING BATTLE,
HENCE YOU AND I CONTINUES TOGETHER.
(HERE YOU REFFERED AS HEART AND ME AS BRAIN.
IT'S A CONFLICT BETWEEN HEART AND BRAIN)

3. You Can't Blame Me

Let me off the hook,
It is me, who can blame me,
Not the eyes which are half blind,
And half that double speaks.
I neither rodomontade
Nor affirm the post truth
So the lips that throb rhythmically,
Dire to get their act together.
Damned if I do and damned if I don't,
They continue to rib off the self alone.
With a dong I'm adhering aloud,
Though it is as setting in stone,
None is allowed to intervene in between
But Deity himself and me of course,
Now concentrate the verse stated before,
As I have had enough of all.

4. Usual Morning

The usual morning from my window,
General happenings are beaded.
Trees are upright having towering stem,
Breezes playing means for leaves
To destined them to their last stop,
Photons strike to silicate panel,
A glazed rend turn up to me,
Pigeons wiping out the stock of straw,
Voices are yet to rise,
But melody has already begun.
Early sun gleaming to enchant
And piercing the ladder
And knocked at my eyes,
Hey there, good morning.

5. You really can't hate

_ Even if you ponder , till the end
you'll come up with loose hand
that vacant space meant to be there
with greys around and nerves filled with tears
but you really can't hate IT
_ Interrogating about the laws won't melt
the commitment your heart hold barely makes sense
whether it's pastoral or royal that define your
living
the flamingo of your mirth flew away
but you really can't hate IT
_ Parallel streets are running with you
willingly wait for emancipation
greens might inundates for now
but you really can't hate IT

6. Query Unresolved

Why my lips flutter,
Every time I encounter a lie?
What is this act
I loathe the moment you disguise?
When am I going to admit,
One is not my cup of tea, is lame?
Where is the route,
To one's mind, that been stated unprecedented?
How come I agreed
That masquerade is the only way to survive?
Who
And I ask who is going to play Divine
To resolve one's problem, if not us?

7. One More Inning

It's drizzling over my shadow,
But I wish to wander more around.
As faults are orphan,
So often made to bound.
You dare to pick the land,
Because what values here is the blue.
Don't shape it in whichever way,
Lord here, is perfect , but are you?
It will shatter you a thousand time
Surrendering isn't a option here in mine.
It is stated that you either be ravenous
Or on fleek for stuffs to be done.
Moreover to be mature enough to endure
The Brownian words that surrounds you once.
Zenith is all you have to achieve.
She got the feather but needs to be cunning
Because the rotten hand doesn't assure
That you get to play ONE MORE INNING....

8. On My Way To Repent

One summer morning,
I deliberately step out,
In the absence of an interlocutor.
It became greasy within a minute
But I continue to paddle thither.
My heart was pounding,
I reticent of former happening
And owe an explanation to myself.
"Either I'll burn bridges,
Or perish existing self honor,
Whichever way I opt, I will left wretched inside,
Plight for a longer time."
With these debate on, exasperated!
I reached my destination and knocked the door .

9. Not Fugitive But Scared

Petrified to even deliver my mind.
Dear, it's not easy for me.
Gain a part of ball is tough though.
It's indecisive for even heaven
Whether to awaken or left
The purpose that holds the cost.
I need to decipher the lingual hidden.
To do so, I have to roughed my bone.
"Is it worthy to bid my blood?"
The other me enquiring aloud.
"It's a requisite deed not a query"
Oh Lord! Finally revealed it out.

10. Musical Soul

The very beginning of emotion,
You draft it into certain frame,
Certain which is not distinctive much,
But is made for the ball is heavenly said
Music is a treatise,
Treatise of words often left unsaid.
Drum beat or chords, sharp or flat,
You hit the notes higher or base,
Whether it is to slur the flute,
Or run your fingers from fret to fret,
Bid your craft to yearning soul,
And earn bliss with no strings attached.
It anyway define music's supremacy
Indeed is an epitome of esstasy.

11. Live Your Life A Moment More

Live your life a moment more,
With a cup of joy in hand
And doubled up for statements present,
Defenestrate your worry and go on,
Blithely live, it's your dorm,
Considering, even if it is not so, a charmed life,
Even with daydream of euphoric one,
You fit the bill, to have it all
Crack up twice on wacky knock,
Don't disguise with mask on,
Berate them, and come along,
Live your life a moment more.

12. I want to live

You dared to cause havoc inside me,
You dared to touch the space within me.
I crossed the path where I bleed to hell.
Plead to live a moment more.
My scream sounds imminent to pinna,
Yet you ask to endure it all.
Justifying this barbarous act
And call yourself a sapiens.
I was left alone in the dark,
Exerting and suffering and abated,
Murmuring inside that I desperately
WANT TO LIVE
WANT TO LIVE.
What sin did this self commit
That my skin scratching
it's tissue to the end.
This red burn slide my hope
To the brink of breath.
Now I'm lying with Lord in heart
Getting short of beats….
Let me survive
My cord wants to scream.

13. I drive since night

Okay I have to state this
I felt like half dead.
It was a call that initiate
From the one residing home away.
Traditionally I had to admit
To reach him in no time.
It was dark swallowed night
With no stars but cloud
Route saying you better reverse,
The thought running your car.
Breezes too couldn't help
But to blow rashly.
Seems it turned out to be a tornado in no time.
Oh thunder,
Take your time to encounter,
My limbs are spelling it out briskly.
Lips, why don't you flutter?
Oh you got jammed, so pity.
Eyes still wishing for crescent to emerge
With these on I way on my way with urge.
A dazzled ray straight from the lobe
Meet the retina picturezes the form.

Oh it's that, my lips throb
That is how I reached my home.

14. I Admit

I am here to admit,
What I was supposed to do
Is not what my path looks like, now.
Consciously or not but I dared to
And traditionally the stated path
Had already been engraved since my first drop.
My worth is yet to be defined,
My alignment towards left,
Finally I accepted to be the one.

15. CRAZYSAURUS

Take your vision and invert it,
Upside down is the phase you click.
She neither snatches nor adds an element,
Bereft of gloom, with aura of crescent,
She happened to be a crazysaurus.
A concoction of winsome and puerile,
Define her and is bonafide.
She spaces out herself but never veg out,
But blessed with a handsome life,
God knows, how?
You need to wrap your head around
To get a piece of persona she has.
A prudent, diligent but colossal sunken soul
Not dime a dozen but crazysaurus she enroll.

16. Complementary Contrast

Why to admit that I can't
When I rather affirm I won't.
Sarcastically fantasizing
For prize to be mine,
But without even a step taken,
I am adjoining it aloud.
Hence it isn't dire to be pious
Moreover in this sucking ride
You got to be driving alone.
So rather pulling up your socks to run
Run to dive in ocean along.

17. Beauty Of Hope

To cut the chase
At the very first place,
It is "Hope" anytime
That makes us breathe.
It's superfluous to invest time
To blame the rotten feet.
It'll smite to hell
If you hooked to repent
No midway on either side
But only hope that glazes.
Deity! You still hold me.
Let me sprout of horizon
Moreover the spell
That let us endeavor,
It is indeed a hope
That left beside
And roars aloud.

18. Dance

Dance is nothing but expressing your emotion.
Neither contriving nor practiced
But flicker over.
Whether it is adversity or
Melancholy, really a big deal,
Dance heals them utterly.
The tip of your toes
Loses contact with the floor,
Arms flung in the air
And make some pattern out of it.
You pop on beat,
Without caring of bloopers,
You raise your feet.
A phase of demure
And pace of abstract frame.
Not only glaring frame with stars stitched
But an austere, not so tidy floor is your stage.
Just put your soul in this and
It'll never let you despair infallibly.
It pours only ebullience not agitation.
And won't let you squall of grief
Or feel tedious but crown you

with serene feel of eternity
And top up with full of life.

19. Beauty Of Nature

That morning,
Full of wavelengths,
With drops like frothy cloud,
And chirping of birds crosses ear,
The sound of feathers,
The way they move,
They woke up so soon.
Picking up straw to hide destitute
From one roof to another,
They fly endless.
Seems so dexterous!
Some flicks, some flares, some flaws,
This chilled comely wind,
When slide on me,
Seems I am diving down,
Not a single apprehension that day.
A leaflet with rachis flowing,
Wants us to apprehend,
What could more lovable than this.
It isn't tedious, isn't impaired,
But full of life and more to have,
It's rational, eternal, lot of reason to love,

That it is, that's the nature.

20. Well Being

When the essence of well being,
Comes to your door,
Your heart itself will pop up,
And coupled to the mind,
Thereafter every conduction exceed,
Limbs therefore wishes to scamper,
Willingly without if and but,
And bank of mirth will become ,
Your next door neighbor.

21. Call Them Friends

Some flaws of mine,
Some suggestions remained,
The perk of mirth,
That naughtiness gave,
Never forsake that hand anyway,
Just rend all vex,
But ribs every day,
They are random creature,
Having weird trait,
Walk with felicity in hand,
On slush that tend,
To pop up heart,
And call them friend.

22. Bride

A sparkling red beauty,
Having blend of emotion inside the veil,
Annulling the figure of numerous remembrance,
Stepping to pave a new way,
The melody of synchronous,
With a bangle hitting the other,
The ornaments are, as if, in a battle,
Who made her comely better?
Some frenetic odd words,
Jammed her encephalon,
She is exhilarate but nervous,
Scratching her soul with absurdity alone.
Her myrtle adopted a random shape,
And eyes reflecting an arcane gay.
Her feet topple quite a time,
But those hands are still awake.

23. The Last Piece Of Cake

In a few meter square,
Cabals gather to celebrate.
One after another,
In a crossway fashion.
Look at those eyes,
Prodigious mirth, vibrating the cord, yeah,
To sing all along, happy birthday.
One can clearly listen to beats,
As no one is in the sink,
It's been quite a time
For main thing to arrive,
Conjecturing that each mind,
Because of this is running wild.
Here you go,
The chocolitious three floored,
With candles on third,
Approaching us on wheel with imperial aura,
She blew it up and minced,
Though each papilla get the taste,
But still precipitancy inside awake,

HARSHITA JAISWAL

Because what left was the,
Last piece of cake.

24. How Am I Suppose To Be

Would this road glance at me,
For a moment or two?
This thing is rushing wild,
And seems as crying for the moon.
Pull yourself together, for me,
Is mere affirmation,
Furthermore I am screaming my heart out.
These letters,
You've got to be shoving off.
This is how it suppose to be,
Nevertheless I got bent out of the shape,
Because this is aching me to hell,
And aiming me to wipe out considering a trash.
Soon this self turn to claustrophobe,
Or antipode but fend the mob,
It's hysterical for me to blame,
But not so, to extract me out.
I'll better be the bone moreover
A suberin in weird drizzle,
Antagonist to what I was a night ago.

A malleable, ductile but not brittle,
This is how I am suppose to be.

25. Welcoming my day

A cup of coffee in one and bunch of books in other,
With headphones on, plucked in pocket,
Feet wore a shoe which is quite worn out,
Wearing printed trouser and T slack,
Eyes deciphering a half sleepy mind,
And feet approaching the ladder,
And swiftly move to terrace.
The moment one drop entered the throat,
It beef up my body immensely,
And I welcome my new day.

26. Are We Still Worthy Of Freedom

Are we worthy of freedom, we possess?
Or we forgo to reflect on toil our people did
Is it still under the weather,
How freedom needs to be treated
It is not, what people believe,
Only celebrating days and people
Overlooking norms, culture,
But valuing sky while residing terra firma
It arises from enlightenment
The values of both the sacrifice and altruistic
But what we do is laxity
Towards upbringing of nation
Or rather state mishandled the leisure of breathing
Though you have freed to pick your version
But don't omit to put glass on wall
And call for reparation to keep freedom precarious
Are we still worthy of this present?

27. I Lost My Journey

I am losing it day by day,
From a picayune to hill.
Is my memory worth oozing,
Amid forlorn ongoing living?
I forfeit the right to hark back,
To my, very own journey, till date.
I often seem to twaddle around,
About reminiscence of past .
I neither have mnemonics to gather
Nor I am a dunderhead
Just dwelling inside a duvet
Of a shadow moving back and forth

28. It's Hysterical, I Back The Wrong Horse

Oh, you drop your words here,
Hysterical, I guess,
But can't move my jewels aside,
Kindly shift your statement to right.
Indebted to clock to remind me awake,
It's fascinating yet duff to darken,
And you too jest high of me.
It's your loss as I am bit witty,
With words and you affirm it's innocuous.
Don't deplore, as you stated
While affixing humor to my work.
Considering this, I am willing
To adjoin, I backed the wrong horse.

29. Stress At Its Peak

Let's call it a day,
I can't move my arms,
It's more of clock,
Than dawn to address,
The load on veins.
Eyes bewails the schedule,
And I am being down in dumps,
Is this the table, I scour for,
Scuffling over tears and tolerance.
Stress up the ewer, but not anymore.
I tricked myself to hit the sack,
And drape this dusk on my lid,
Brush the task off my shoulder,
Cause stress is dwelling at its peak.

30. Ground Zero

Even today,
I left out in the cloud.
So let's slide back to the row
And pull off the skill all over.
Embrace it or not,
I'll keep on putting an arm.
Of course, I firmed my fist
To clench the breeze, approaching others.
I tapped twice and left cooling my heels.
But keeping my head on spikes,
Reflects me as dunce as
Icing sun in the core.
That's the turn make me sprint
To catch the plumes and cling to it.

31. I Am a Bubble

I am a bubble
And a daydreamer, if I retort.
Not much of me is hidden
And spiking off the reflection.
I exist on the layer
And cremate in its core.
I am a crate of ebullience,
Residing in crevasse alone.
I don't happen to be crony,
Moreover own a frail frame.
But revealing myself to be foxy,
I meant to play the rain.

32. Exist As a woman

Charge them a big time,
To exist as a woman.
And coronet all,
To shadow down to toe,
For throng, hardly give a knock.
It's derogatory with a bang.
Have you descried the seed?
They owe an ovation, don't they?
Apotheosis of living,
You must be jesting.
Are they felon or else
Why would have they been sentenced
To dash to other's pace
It's a palpable sense of demeaning
Oneself, in dark with grace.

33. Living on My Own

It's been a while,
You have to shot.
You brutally denied,
My consideration for you.
It was once a dream,
To picture us perfectly, somewhere.
But not anymore,
As it was to be done.
I'm no more afraid of losing one,
I'm not afraid to shatter down,
I'm not drunk to ride alone,
"Living on my own"
"Living on my own."
You took your hand
Off my neck
To shake me well till the end.
Neither I'm a victim,
Nor you are wrong.
It's matter of choice
That we made on our own.
It drives me crazy as how come?
Once and for all it's already done.

It pushes me off the brink of cliff.
But I'm,
"Living on my own"
"Living on my own."

34. You Step Up

You step up,
Step up to clench the moment.
But failed twice
As bug in current.
Entwines with determination
In hand.
Took few steps back,
Just to take a leap of faith,
With usual bitsy in your pocket,
Promised never to get slackened.
You might be obscured,
Hitherto! Nothing procured.
But footsteps kept on chasing,
The aim that you adhered.
Silt all around,
With layers in between,
Only pebbles embedded,
But need not to scream.
Embrace the entire gap
And build your own
Delineated avenue to left the trail.
Surely, will declare the triumph,

HARSHITA JAISWAL

At the end of the day.

35. Where I Can Exist

Where lips aren't sealed
And life is abstract itsy.
Where breathing is engraved with sapphires
And system holds the definition nothing.
Where hands aren't confined to columns
And galaxies are the only limit.
Where the aroma of acme isn't paramount
And flaws are enclasp and admire.
Where dawn never follows dusk
And sin hit nihility.
A sphere where I can exist, off handcuffs
And paint the town red with no rows mentioned.

36. A Limerick

I, with a plucky heart, went to attempt pizzicato alone,
As soon as I held violin, clavicle yelped in ludicrous tone,
Down-bow staccato, was what I chose first,
Literally, planning to make ears bleed to worst,
And I left with a warning, never to approach even on
phone.

37. Then I'll give away my tears

When the sky drops its angel
And acanthus halts absorbing.
When the portals open to repine
And forgiving become the apex of ease.
When talisman, in sooth, brings a stroke of luck
And merriment is the only gospel of existence.
When misdemeanor surrenders first
And paradise offers its serenity.
When tides sit on breeze
And sword stated flotsam while on chariot.
Then I'll give away my tears
With fervent harmony.

38. Let's Steal Ourselves from Us

Let's ride to the shore that stays quiet,
Cross the boscage with utmost tranquility,
Where there is no route and no destiny
Only mellifluous music of streams,
Escorting me on feet, with breeze being frosty.
Let's walk under the quilt of clouds,
Far from chaos, with no man but nature alone.
Where paradise incarnates and spells begin.
The path that defines itself with sheath of turf
And cobble enveloped with dew, dares you,
Let's steal ourselves from us
And devote to divinity of the circumambient.

39. She Recedes Far in the Dark

An ardent believer of life
To be smooth on desk and not bumpy.
She was a valiant with dorsum, peerless
And herself accentuate on dignity, she entitled,
Never went off the rails moreover toiled to exist.
Verily she didn't possess but was the pace.
It beats me as how,
All at once, existence hops in dusk? Now
What shore has, is shade diffused and follows,
Only quilt of scorch and laceration on her.
She is defying holding on to herself
And her psyche couldn't knock to bawl.
It isn't that she is muddle headed
But it's the temper that chose to tremor.
She neither welcoming nor approaching
Her entity and recedes far in the dark.

40. Hold of Your Existence

This is nth time am reminding
You to exist all over again
Or evolve if you wish to
But don't pick a bolt hole.
Either be a tenant to being or
Own your globe, your call.
Save your skin, hold your opulence
Whatsoever it takes I am willing to.
Let's affix our frontiers, I am
Offering my entity, cutaneous to marrow
Or to each string, every matter that entails.
Holding out with you, defunct, is insatiate.
Even if you wish, just drop by
Or stay cheek by jowl in our sojoum
But do lay hold of your existence.

41. Hold of Your Existence

This is nth time am reminding
You to exist all over again
Or evolve if you wish to
But don't pick a bolt hole.
Either be a tenant to being or
Own your globe, your call.
Save your skin, hold your opulence
Whatsoever it takes I am willing to.
Let's affix our frontiers, I am
Offering my entity, cutaneous to marrow
Or to each string, every matter that entails.
Holding out with you, defunct, is insatiate.
Even if you wish, just drop by
Or stay cheek by jowl in our sojoum
But do lay hold of your existence.

42. I Chose a Particular Lingo

43. Art of Disguise

*They somehow managed to master the art of dwelling
inside,
A penny more an asset less, anyway nullify the street wild,
No more acceptance of grotesque, forgiving is the farthest
stop,
Sophistry is where they excel; furthermore it is wit that
drives.
Ocean sprinted to bounce back and tide riding it to
survive,
They are at shore to adsorb its firm and mask on to
deceive,
There is nothing as crystal in the sphere where they exist,
Rubies here are fragile shadow layered with reflection's
web,
Because foyer to zenith is offer to one who can disguise
himself.*

44. Don't Find Me

I am rolling out,
It's all dark around
With miniscule voices guiding
And no man behind and following.
I am bleeding blue but nowhere
Is the destiny I chose.
Fortunately, still one more
Breath is left, but I am falling
Into the fall and failed
To approach myself.
I am pleading to find
Me never, if possible, I
Would like to escape
Once again

45. Voice of Street

You adjoin a bit less
What left is me as trash
Chase until it's yours
Is the only alarm, we set
Threat, not an opinion, bold
And firm in core and foam
As sheath, a remnant
Retch all, my inn has
My restive being, reminisce
Unit para and quickly get back
As I am not a highbrow
And not benighted too if affirm
I bemoaned for the differences
A Street and a lane faces.

About The Book

"Verses' Ladder, Rhythm beaded in words" is a shelf of verses that defines the beauty of writing your mind in the form of poetry written by Harshita Jaiswal. Each poetry is straight from her heart through her pen. This book addresses the narrative of emotion, music, dance, health, elated living and many more. The beauty of poetry is inevitable and takes few stances to explain. This piece of writing will take you to the hemisphere of a person's aspects of living whether it is going to repent, bleeding heart or having a cup of joy and living life a bit more.

About The Author

Harshita Jaiswal, a student adopted writing as a part of her living. "Verses' Ladder, Rhythm beaded in words" is her debut book as an author. Her preferred form is poetry as she believes "poetry is nothing but beading emotion into words exactly as music." Rhythm binds people more often .